In the Know

INFLUENCERS AND TRENDS

FASHION

Virginia Loh-Hagan

45TH PARALLEL PRESS

Published in the United States of America by Cherry Lake Publishing Group
Ann Arbor, Michigan
www.cherrylakepublishing.com

Reading Adviser: Marla Conn, MS, Ed., Literacy specialist, Read-Ability, Inc.
Book Designer: Felicia Macheske

Photo Credits: © AlexAnnaButs/Shutterstock, cover; © aiaikawa/Shutterstock, cover; © vuvu/Shutterstock, 1; © Public Domain/pxhere, 4; © karnizz/Shutterstock, 7; © carballo/Shutterstock, 8; © Surf Stories/Shutterstock, 10; © Alena Ozerova/Shutterstock, 12; © Kiselev Andrey Valerevich/Shutterstock, 15; © Look Studio/Shutterstock, 16; © ax_tanyatanya/Shutterstock, 18; © Satya Putra/Shutterstock, 20; © gmn /Shutterstock, 22; © Vergani Fotografia/Shutterstock, 23; © Library of Congress/Photograph by Harris & Ewing/LOC Control No.: 2016883387, 24; © FashionStock.com/Shutterstock, 26; © lev radin/Shutterstock, 28; © Evgeniya Porechenskaya/Shutterstock, 31

45th Parallel Press is an imprint of Cherry Lake Publishing Group.

Library of Congress Cataloging-in-Publication Data

Names: Loh-Hagan, Virginia, author.
Title: Fashion / Virginia Loh-Hagan.
Description: Ann Arbor : Cherry Lake Publishing, 2021. | Series: In the know: influencers and trends | Includes index. | Summary: "We're spilling the tea on the latest trends. Curious about the lives of influencers? Want to know more about VSCO girls or sustainable fashion? Read more to be in the know. This high-interest series is written at a low readability to aid struggling readers. Each book includes educational sidebars, throwback biographies of "OG" influencers, fast facts, and social media challenges, as well as a table of contents, glossary of keywords, index, and author biography"— Provided by publisher.
Identifiers: LCCN 2020032483 (print) | LCCN 2020032484 (ebook) | ISBN 9781534180338 (hardcover) | ISBN 9781534182042 (paperback) | ISBN 9781534181342 (pdf) | ISBN 9781534183056 (ebook)
Subjects: LCSH: Fashion—Juvenile literature. | Clothing and dress—Juvenile literature. | Sustainable design—Juvenile literature.
Classification: LCC GT518 .L654 2021 (print) | LCC GT518 (ebook) | DDC 391—dc23
LC record available at https://lccn.loc.gov/2020032483
LC ebook record available at https://lccn.loc.gov/2020032484

Cherry Lake Publishing Group would like to acknowledge the work of the Partnership for 21st Century Learning, a Network of Battelle for Kids. Please visit *http://www.battelleforkids.org/networks/p21* for more information.

Printed in the United States of America
Corporate Graphics

Dr. Virginia Loh-Hagan is an author, university professor, and former classroom teacher. She loves wearing dresses with pockets. She lives in San Diego with her very tall husband and very naughty dogs.

Companies love influencers. They use them to promote their products.

Introduction

What's **trending**? What's in? What's not? Trends are popular fads. They're widely talked about. They **dominate** the internet. Dominate means to rule over.

Influencers are people who set trends. They post a lot on **social media**. Social media are online communication platforms used to share information. Influencers post photos and videos. They post blogs and stories. They inspire a **following**. Following refers to fans. Fans make trends come to life. They spread trends. They make trends popular.

Some trends stick. Some trends don't. This book explores trends in fashion. Fashion means clothing styles.

Just like you have a certain style, there are different styles for each culture. Even different time periods have specific styles. What was trending in the early 2000s might not be trending today. But sometimes trends can come back. There have been many fashion trends. And there will continue to be many more.

In the past, people looked to kings and queens for fashion trends.

Today, people look to fashion influencers. Fashion influencers post content about clothes. They post content about **accessories**. Accessories include shoes, hats, and jewelry.

Fashion influencers create their own style. They create bold looks. They create fresh looks. Influencers inspire their followers. Followers copy their looks.

Fashion is more than just about clothes. Some people think fashion is an art. Some people think fashion sends messages. They think fashion can create an impact. It can change the world.

The COVID-19 pandemic influenced fashion trends, popularizing colorful and unique nonmedical masks. ▸

There are many shopping apps and profiles that support sustainable fashion, like Depop, Poshmark, and Mercari.

CHAPTER 1

Sustainable Fashion

Sustainable fashion is a hot trend. Sustainable means saving natural resources. It means helping the environment.

Sustainable fashion fans avoid fast fashion. Fast fashion refers to clothes made cheaply and quickly. These clothes are made in large amounts. They copy the latest fashion styles.

Instead, sustainable fashion fans support slow fashion. Slow fashion is about making and buying clothes that last a long time. They re-wear old clothes. They **upcycle**. Upcycle means adding new designs to old clothes. Sustainable fashion is eco-friendly.

Celebrities are known to support sustainable fashion. Emma Watson wears and supports eco-friendly and sustainable clothing. Billie Eilish launched a clothing brand in early 2020. She wanted to design clothes that were both affordable and sustainable. Celebrities do this to set an example for their fans.

Marina Testino is a fashion influencer. She started the #OneDressToImpress project. She wore the same red suit every day. She did this for 2 months. She also started the #CarryOnSummer project. She traveled in Europe with only a small suitcase.

Sustainable fashion fans swap clothes. They buy used clothes. They only buy fair fashion. Fair fashion requires workers to be paid enough money to have basic needs.

Emma Slade Edmondson has an IGTV series. This series is called *Come* **Secondhand** *Shopping with Me*. Secondhand means used. Edmondson also founded **Charity** Fashion Live. Charity refers to donations. Edmondson created a fashion show with models wearing used clothes.

◀ Many sustainable fashion fans believe in making eco-friendly choices in all aspects of life.

VSCO girls like reusable straws and water bottles. They care about Earth and its animals.

CHAPTER 2

"It" Girls and Boys

"It" girls and boys are super popular people. They have fame and beauty. They're influencers. Over time, there have been different "It" looks.

VSCO refers to Visual Supply Company. VSCO is an app that allows users to edit photos and videos. Users can share these edited photos and videos in the app. They can also share it to other social media platforms. The "VSCO girl" look is basic. It's laid-back. It's beachy. Fans of the VSCO girl look sometimes wear **crop** tops. Crop means cut short. They sometimes wear oversized shirts. They like jean shorts. They can be seen wearing shell necklaces. They sport friendship bracelets. Their water bottles are covered in stickers. They wear scrunchies on their wrists and in their hair. Some say the VSCO girl look is a **throwback** to the 90s. Throwbacks are reminders of the past.

BE A LITTLE EXTRA

SOCIAL MEDIA CHALLENGE

Create a lookbook on Instagram. Lookbooks are collections of photos. They show off different outfits. They're like fashion catalogs. They're like fashion diaries.

Decide the theme of your lookbook. An example is party outfits. Another example is hiking outfits.

Include a cover page. This page should state the theme.

Dress from head to toe. Include headwear. Include jewelry. Include shoes.

Take good photos. Include entire outfits. Take vertical photos. Vertical means upright.

Model the clothes. Strike a simple pose.

Take close-up photos of special features. Special features could be stitching.

Leave out costs. Leave out brand names. Just focus on visuals.

Think about what you'll write in your caption. Maybe include what inspired the outfits.

Instead of Instagram, use TikTok. Look up fashion challenges to try.

"Wallpaper Girls" live in big, trendy cities like Los Angeles, California, or New York City, New York. They take selfies in front of fancy wallpaper. They mix fancy and non-fancy things together. Iris Apatow is the daughter of a famous movie director. She's known as a Wallpaper Girl.

"E-Girl Factory" TikTok videos were popular in early 2019. Girls posted videos of themselves transforming into e-girls. Then, boys started doing it. Now, e-girls and e-boys are popular looks. "E" stands for electronic. E-girls and e-boys have bright dyed hair. They wear dark eyeliner. They draw small shapes under their eyes. They wear pink blush. They wear chains as jewelry. They may have fake freckles. They like gaming.

E-girls and e-boys dress a lot like goths. Goths are connected to punk rock.

Mom jeans and dad jeans are high-waisted.

CHAPTER 3

Throwback Fashion

Throwback fashion trends are also called **nostalgic** fashion. Nostalgia is a longing for the past. It's also called **retro** fashion. Retro means going back in time. People find comfort in trends from the past. They find it familiar. They find it safe. Teenagers can raid their parents' closets to find throwback fashion gems.

Specifically, fashion from the 1980s, 1990s, and 2000s are coming back. There are many examples. Mom and dad jeans are back. Fanny packs are back. Tie-dye is back. Band tees are back. Chunky tennis shoes are back. Bright, neon colors are back.

Some people specialize in **vintage** fashion. Vintage means something made in the past. It includes clothes, makeup, and hairstyles.

Nora Thoeng is better known as Nora Finds. She's a scientist. She's also a vintage clothing expert. Her love of vintage clothes started at age 9. Her Instagram posts include photos of her wearing clothes from the 1930s to 1950s. She said, "My love of vintage stems from my love of history and stories behind every piece, so the blog is dedicated to telling stories and connecting with people who want to know about me and my outfits."

◀ Many people who love vintage fashion go thrifting. Thrifting is shopping at thrift stores.

Customized outfits start conversations. The idea is to get people to ask, "Where did you get that?"

CHAPTER 4

DIY Fashion

DIY is another trend. DIY means do it yourself.

People are encouraged to add personality to clothes. Edie Campbell is a model. She partnered with Christabel MacGreevy. MacGreevy is her childhood friend. She's an illustrator. Campbell and MacGreevy started a company. They reuse fabrics. They design pictures. They make pictures into patches. People can buy the patches and sew them onto their clothes.

Customizing outfits makes clothes unique. Customize means to change to fit one's style. People add big buttons to dresses. They add feathers to shoes. They add tassels to skirts. They add jewelry to jeans, purses, and shoes.

Spilling the TEA

FASHION INFLUENCERS

Did you know...

- Queen Victoria ruled England. She lived from 1819 to 1901. She's believed to have started two big trends. She wore white on her wedding day. Today, brides wear white dresses. When her husband died, she wore black. Today, people wear black to honor those who died.

- Chinami Mori is a fashion designer. She makes colorful scarves. Her grandmother is named Emiko. Emiko is 93 years old. She models Mori's scarves. Mori posts pictures of Emiko wearing the scarves. She does this on Instagram. She has over 45,000 followers. Mori said, "She's my favorite person in the whole world."

- Chiara Ferragni is Italian. She's a fashion blogger. She's a fashion designer. She's one of the world's top fashion influencers. She has over 19 million followers. During the 2020 pandemic, she shared her "house outfits." She raised money for Italian hospitals. She said, "I'm trying my best to help my country."

Making your own clothes is trendy now too. Sam Nowell is a fashion designer. His friend taught him how to sew. He also used YouTube to build his skills. He makes clothes from fabric trash. He turns towels into pants. He turns shower curtains into jackets.

Haute couture means high fashion. It dominates the fancy fashion shows. It's known for being over the top. A popular trend is #HomeCouture. People re-create the fancy fashion designs. They use household things. George Serventi is a fashion journalist. He started the trend. He copied a fashion look. He used puffed-up white trash bags. He encouraged others to do the same. The idea is to get people to create.

▲ Making your own unique nonmedical mask was a popular trend during the COVID-19 pandemic.

In 1933, Eleanor Roosevelt was the first First Lady to wear pants at a formal event.

CHAPTER 5

Androgynous Fashion

Evita Nuh has over 73,000 followers. She started blogging at age 8. She did this as a way to talk to people. She has **Asperger's syndrome**. People with Asperger's have a hard time talking to others.

Nuh has a unique style. She created her own DIY fashion brand. She said, "The rule is no rules!" She loves "wearing boys' stuff."

Nuh embraces **androgyny**. Androgynous fashion aims to avoid gender stereotypes. It aims to look neither like a boy nor a girl. It aims to blend different styles.

Designers of androgynous fashion work hard to make clothes as comfortable as men's clothing. They also want to make clothes as stylish as women's clothing.

Jenn Im is a fashion influencer. She has a YouTube channel. She has over 2.7 million subscribers. She has over 1.7 million followers on Instagram. She has almost 200,000 followers on Twitter. In 2017, she started her own fashion company. She called it Eggie. Eggie featured Im's Korean heritage. It also featured **gender-neutral** clothes. Gender-neutral means it can be worn by both men and women. Im said, "It was important for me to create some pieces in the collection that were gender-neutral because style is more fluid than ever and should be inclusive for all." Inclusive means open to everyone.

◄ Both men and women can wear pantsuits.

There are size-inclusive runway shows during fashion week.

CHAPTER

6

Plus-Size Fashion

People come in all shapes and sizes. Fashion should be for everyone. In the past, only certain-sized models would be part of fashion shows. This is changing. More **plus-size** outfits are being included in shows. Plus-size refers to clothes that are larger.

Jessica Torres is a plus-size fashion influencer. She co-hosts a podcast called *Fat Girls Club*. She has her own YouTube channel called ThisIsJessicaTorres. She describes herself as "a plus-size Latina from the Bronx who just wanted to wear cute clothes." She wears crop tops. She wears bikinis. She doesn't hide her body. She embraces it.

THROWBACK

OG INFLUENCER

There were influencers before social media. An original (or "OG") fashion influencer was Jacqueline Kennedy Onassis (1929–1994). She was called "Jackie O" for short. She was the wife of President John F. Kennedy. She was known as the First Lady of Fashion. After Kennedy died, she married Aristotle Onassis. She influenced millions of women around the world. Women everywhere copied her look. Onassis was known for being elegant. She set many trends. She had a signature look. She was known for wearing pearls, white gloves, a pillbox hat, and a tailored skirt-suit. Tailored means designed to fit her body. Pillbox hats are small hats. They have flat tops. They have straight sides. Onassis started many other fashion trends. She wore fancy scarves. She wore scarves on her head. She wore big sunglasses. She wore strapless gowns. She wore bows on her waist. She wore capes. She wore coats. She wore horse-riding boots. She wore all-white clothes.

Chastity Garner Valentine and CeCe Olisa are plus-size fashion influencers. They started a conference for the plus-size fashion community. The event is called "The Curvy Con." It gives plus-size shoppers a special experience. It makes them feel special.

Michael-Anthony Spearman is known as "The Big Fashion Guy." He's a plus-size male fashion influencer. He's the king of suits. He likes to mix colors, patterns, and fabrics. He also loves to wear hats. He wants to design stylish clothes for big and tall gentlemen. He said, "What I want big and tall men to learn from my brand is that you can do or wear whatever a smaller guy is wearing and even look better while doing it."

▲ More and more companies are expanding their size range to be more size-inclusive.

Glossary

accessories (ak-SES-ur-eez) fashion items added to an outfit, like shoes, hats, and jewelry

androgyny (an-DRAH-juh-nee) being neither male nor female

Asperger's syndrome (AHS-pur-gurz SIN-drohm) a developmental disorder that causes people to have difficulty with social interactions

charity (CHAR-ih-tee) the giving of help, money, or goods to those in need

crop (KRAHP) cut short

customizing (KUHS-tuh-mize-ing) changing in order to fit one's style

dominate (DAH-muh-nate) to rule over

following (FAH-loh-ing) fans or supporters

gender-neutral (JEN-dur NOO-truhl) designed for both males and females

haute couture (OHT koo-TOOR) high fashion

influencers (IN-floo-uhns-urz) people who set trends by posting a lot on social media and have large followings

nostalgic (nah-STAL-jik) having a longing for the past

plus-size (PLUHS SIZE) size that is larger

retro (RET-roh) going back in time

secondhand (SEK-uhnd-hand) previously used

social media (SOH-shuhl MEE-dee-uh) online communications used to share information

sustainable (suh-STAY-nuh-buhl) done in a way that can be continued and that doesn't use up natural resources

throwback (THROH-bak) reminder of the past

trending (TREND-ing) currently a popular fad online

upcycle (UHP-sye-kuhl) to change something to produce something that is better than the original

vintage (VIN-tij) something made long ago

Learn More

Croll, Jennifer, and Aneta Pacholska (illust.). *Bad Boys of Fashion: Style Rebels and Renegades Through the Ages*. Toronto, ON: Annick Press, 2019.

Loh-Hagan, Virginia. *Far Out Fashion*. Ann Arbor, MI: Cherry Lake Publishing, 2018.

Sedlackova, Jana. *The Complete Book of Fashion History: A Stylish Journey Through History and the Ultimate Guide for Being Fashionable in Every Era*. Mission Viejo, CA: Walter Foster Jr., 2017.

Index